Inspired
by Nature

Inspired
by Nature

edited by
Amy Kelley

FALCON®

Cover illustrations by Peter Grosshauser.

Text illustrations by Amy Kelley unless otherwise noted.

Grateful acknowledgment is made to those who granted permission to reprint the selections in this book. A complete list of copyright permissions can be found on the following two pages.

Cataloging-in-Publication Data is on record at the Library of Congress.

Acknowledgments

"The Heat Of Noon: Rock, Tree And Cloud" from *Desert Solitaire: A Season in the Wilderness* by Edward Abbey. Reprinted by permission of Don Congdon Associates, Inc. Copyright © 1968 by Edward Abbey, renewed 1996 by Clarke Abbey.

"The One-Inch Journey" from *The Unforseen Wilderness: Kentucky's Red River Gorge* by Wendell Berry. Copyright © 1991 by Wendell Berry. Reprinted by permission of North Point Press, a division of Farrar, Straus & Giroux, Inc.

"Teaching a Stone to Talk: Expeditions and Encounters" from *Teaching a Stone to Talk* by Annie Dillard. Copyright © 1982 by Annie Dillard. Reprinted by permission of HarperCollins Publishers, Inc.

"Looking for a Lost Dog" from *Islands, The Universe, Home* by Gretel Ehrlich. Copyright © 1991 by Gretel Ehrlich. Used by permission of Viking Penguin, a division of Penguin Putnam, Inc.

"Angler" from *On the Road with Charles Kuralt* by Charles Kuralt, CBS Inc. Copyright © 1985 by CBS Inc. Used by permission of Putnam Berkley, a division of Penguin Putnam Inc.

"March" from *A Sand County Almanac: And Sketches Here and There* by Aldo Leopold. Copyright © 1949, 1977 by Oxford Press, Inc. Used by permission of Oxford Press, Inc.

Contents

Introduction

Working on this collection allowed my imagination to escape the confines of my studio apartment in Portland, Oregon. I had just moved from Montana, where the outdoors was very much a part of my daily life and inspiration, to attend art school. The apartment felt unbearably small, dark, and cold during those rainy winter months; I was often homesick for Montana's blue skies.

When not struggling through art assignments, this project led me to seek refuge in the downtown public library. The library was a retreat—warm and welcoming and full of *stuff*. Sometimes I would lose track of time, title-jumping in some new section, wandering down a new aisle. It felt like blazing trail, following leads from friends and family. I would stuff my backpack, ride my bike home through the drizzle, and unload my catch on the bed, which occupied three-fourths of my room.

In the aura of reading, I'd realize I didn't feel cold anymore. Edward Abbey took me to the Utah desert at high noon. Gretel Ehrlich had me floating on my back in the middle of a warm summer lake. Wallace Stegner brought back warm memories of hiking across the Grand Canyon with my best friend. Nearly every author made me feel that I was not so far from Montana after all.

Now, I have the opportunity to share with you a few gems that I hope will provide inspiration on an outdoor adventure, or an opportunity for you to share in turn with friends or family. That's what I had in mind, that these pieces would be read aloud around the campfire or during a lunch stop on the trail.

It's a hodgepodge collection, but it has a purpose. In choosing each piece I thought of those nonessentials that you might stuff into your pack at the last minute: the deck of cards, the Frisbee, the rain poncho. The kind of things that can be lifesavers—or at least experience-enhancers. Perhaps you will run across a sentence or paragraph that reminds you of an experience long ago. Perhaps you will be transported to someplace completely different. Perhaps you will simply look a little more closely at the place where you are. Or, perhaps you will just be making good use of those last few minutes with the flashlight before snuggling down in your bag.

Enjoy.

p.s. Many thanks to Erin Turner, my editor, for holding my hand through this adventure, and to Cathy and Mom and other friends who will see their influence in the selections.

Edward Abbey

From "The Heat of Noon: Rock and Tree and Cloud"
in *Desert Solitaire: A Season in the Wilderness*

The sun reigns, I am drowned in light. At this hour, sitting alone at the focal point of the universe, surrounded by a thousand square miles of largely uninhabited no-man's-land—or all-men's-land—I cannot seriously be disturbed by any premonitions of danger to my vulnerable wilderness or my all-too-perishable republic. All dangers seem equally remote. In this glare of brilliant emptiness, in this arid intensity of pure heat, in the heart of a weird solitude, great silence and grand desolation, all things recede to distances out of reach, reflecting light but impossible to touch, annihilating all thought and all that men have made to a spasm of whirling dust far out on the golden desert.

The flowers that graced the red dunes in April

and May have withered now, all gone to seed except for a few drooping sunflowers. The cliffrose has faded, the yucca stalks have bloomed, blown, died, cracked and dried, the seedpods now only empty husks. Under the daily sweep of the parching May winds almost everything that was green has been burned to soft, sere tones of saffron and auburn. But the summer thunderstorms have not yet begun. When they come, as they soon will, we'll see a resurgence of hairy green across the land—the succulent scratchy allergenic tumbleweed, that exotic import from the Mongolian steppes.

The majority of living things retreat before the stunning glare and heat of midday. A snake or lizard exposed to the noon sun for more than ten minutes would die; having no internal cooling mechanism the reptiles must at all costs avoid extremes of temperature, especially in the desert where the temperature on the surface of the ground is much higher than it is in the air a few feet above. The snakes therefore seek shade, waiting until sundown to come out to hunt for supper. The insect-eating lizards dart from shelter to shelter, never lingering for more than a few moments in the open blaze.

The other creatures do the same. Like myself, they stay in the shade as much as possible. To conserve bodily moisture and energy the rodents remain in their burrows during the day. Scorpions and spiders go underground for the duration. Deer, antelope, bighorn sheep, bobcats, foxes and coyotes all shade up beneath rock ledges, oakbrush, pinyon and juniper trees, till the sun goes down.

Even the red ants keep to the inside of their evil nests at noon, though they will come spilling out eager to fight if riled with a stick—I've tried it, naturally.

Flowers curl up. Leaves fold inward. Everything shrinks, contracts, shrivels; somewhere, a desiccated limb on an ancient dying cottonwood tree splits off from the trunk, and the rending fibers make a sound like the shriek of a woman.

The birds are muted, inactive. Now and then I can hear the faraway call of a mourning dove—a call that always sounds far away. A few gray desert sparrows fly from one tree to the next, stop there, do not reappear. The ravens and magpies stay in the shade, the former up on the rimrock, the latter in the trees. The owls, of course, and the nighthawks keep to holes and crevices during the day.

Insect life, sparse to begin with on the open desert, diminishes to near total invisibility and inaudibility during the heat of the day, although at times, during the very hottest and stillest hour, you may hear the eerie ticking noise of a sun-demented cricket or locust, a small sad music that seems to have—like a Bach partita—a touch of something ageless, out of time, eternal in its primeval vibrations.

In this static period even the domestic livestock—horses, sheep, goats, cattle—have sense enough to take it easy, relaxing in the shade. Of all the featherless beasts only man, chained by his self-imposed slavery to the clock, denies the elemental fire and proceeds as best he can about his business, suffering quietly, martyr to his madness. Much to learn.

Among the wild things only the hawks, vultures and eagles seem to remain fully active during the hottest days and hottest hours of the desert. I have seen them circling and soaring far in the sky at high noon, dark wings against the blue, above the heat.

What are they doing up there in the middle of

the sky at the apex of the day? I watch them for hour after hour with the naked eye and with binoculars and never see either hawk or eagle stoop and strike at such a time. And no wonder, for there's precious little fresh meat abroad. Nor does the buzzard descend for lunch or make any effort of any kind. The hawks appear most frequently and most briefly, gliding overhead on some invisible stream in the air. The golden eagle does not come into sight often but stays longer than the hawk, floating toward the horizon in overlapping circles until out of sight.

The vulture or buzzard, master of soaring flight, is most common and most often seen. He stays aloft for hours at a time without ever stirring his long black white-trimmed wings, recognizable at a great distance by their dihedral inclination. Never in a hurry to get anywhere or do anything, an indolent and contemplative bird, he hovers on a thermal, rocking slightly, rising slowly, slips off, sails forward and upward without lifting a feather, primaries extended like fingers at his wingtips. He soars around and around in expanding spirals, lingering at a thousand feet above the landscape, bleak eyes missing nothing that moves below. Or maybe—who can be sure?—he is fast asleep up there, dreaming of a previous incarnation when wings were only a dream. Still without a stroke the vulture rises higher, higher, in ever wider circles, until nothing can be seen of this gaunt, arrogant, repellent bird but the coal-dark V-sign of his wings against the blue dome of heaven.

Around noon the heat waves begin flowing upward from the expanses of sand and bare rock. They shimmer like transparent, filmy veils between my sanctuary in the shade and all the sun-dazzled world beyond. Objects and forms viewed through this tremulous flow appear somewhat displaced or distorted, as a stick seems bent when half-immersed in water.

The great Balanced Rock floats a few inches above its pedestal, supported by a layer of super-heated air. The buttes, pinnacles and fins in the Windows area bend and undulate beyond the middle ground like a painted backdrop stirred by a draft of air. The peaks of the Sierra La Sal—Mount Nass, Mount Tomaski, Mount Peale, Mount Tukuhnikivats and the others—seem to melt into one another, merging like cloud forms so that the profile of one mountain cannot be distinguished from that of another closer or farther away.

In the foreground the dwarf trees of pinyon pine and juniper waver like algae under water without, however, losing any of their sharpness of detail. There is in fact no illusion of the sort called mirage, only the faint deception of motion where nothing is actually moving but the overheated air. You are not likely to see a genuine mirage on the high desert of canyon and mesa country; for that spectacle we must go west or southwest into the basin-and-range provinces of Arizona, Nevada, Southern California and Sonora. There the dry lake beds between the parallel mountain ranges fill with planes of hot air which reflect sky and mountains in mirror fashion, creating the illusory lakes of blue water, the inverted mountains, the strange vision of men and animals walking through or upon water—Palestinian miracles.

Dehydration: the desert air sucks moisture from every pore. I take a drink from the canvas waterbag dangling near my head, the water cooled by evaporation. Noontime here is like a drug. The light is psychedelic, the dry electric air narcotic. To me the desert is stimulating, exciting, exacting; I feel no temptation to sleep or to relax into occult dreams but rather an opposite effect which sharpens and heightens vision, touch, hearing, taste and smell. Each stone, each plant, each grain of sand exists in and for itself with a clarity that is undimmed by any suggestion of a different realm. *Claritas, integritas, veritas.* Only the sunlight holds things together. Noon is the crucial hour: the desert reveals itself nakedly and cruelly, with no meaning but its own existence.

My lone juniper stands half-alive, half-dead, the silvery wind-rubbed claw of wood projected stiffly at the sun. A single cloud floats in the sky to the northeast, motionless, a magical coalescence of vapor where a few minutes before there was nothing visible but the hot, deep, black-grained blueness of infinity.

Life has come to a standstill, at least for the hour. In this forgotten place the tree and I wait on the shore of time, temporarily free from the force of motion and process and the surge toward—what? Something called the *future*? I am free, I am compelled, to contemplate the world which underlies life, struggle, thought, ideas, the human labyrinth of hope and despair.

Through half-closed eyes, for the light would otherwise be overpowering, I consider the tree, the lonely cloud, the sandstone bedrock of this part of the world and pray—in my fashion—for a vision of truth. I listen for signals from the sun—but that distant music is too high and pure for the human ear. I gaze at the tree and receive no response. I scrape my bare feet against the sand and rock under the table and am comforted by their solidity and resistance. I look at the cloud.

Wendell Berry

From "The One-Inch Journey" in
The Unforeseen Wilderness:
Kentucky's Red River Gorge

The mollusk-shell of our civilization, in which we more and more completely enclose ourselves, is lined on the inside with a nacreous layer that is opaque, rainbow-tinted, and an inch thick. It is impossible to see through it to the world; it works, rather, as a reflecting surface upon which we cast the self-flattering outlines and the optimistic tints of our preconceptions of what the world is.

These obscuring preconceptions were once superstitious or religious. Now they are mechanical. The figure representative of the earlier era was that of the otherworldly man who thought and said much more about where he would go when he died than about where he was living. Now we have the figure of the tourist-photographer who, one gathers, will never know where he is, but only, in looking at his pictures, where he *was*. Between his eye and the world is interposed the mechanism of the camera—and also, perhaps, the mechanism of economics: having bought the camera, he has to keep using it to get his money's worth. For him the camera will never work as an instrument of perception or discovery. Looking through it, he is not likely to see anything that will surprise or delight or frighten him, or change his sense of things. As he uses it, the camera is in bondage to the self-oriented assumptions that thrive within the social enclosure. It is an extension of his living room in which his pictures will finally be shown. And if you think the aspect or the atmosphere of his living room might be changed somewhat by the pictures of foreign places and wonders that he has visited, then look, won't you, at the pictures themselves. He has photographed only what he has been prepared to see by other people's photographs. He has gone religiously and taken a picture of what he saw pictured in the travel brochures before he left home. He has photographed scenes that he could have bought on postcards or prepared slides at the nearest drug store, the major difference being the frequent appearance in his photographs of himself, or his wife and kids. He poses the members of his household on the brink of a canyon that the wind and water have been carving at for sixty million years as if there were an absolute equality between them, as if there were no precipice for the body and no abyss for the mind. And before he leaves he adds to the view his empty film cartons and the ruins of his picnic. He is blinded by the device by which he has sought to preserve his vision. He has, in effect, been no place and seen nothing; awesomest wonders rest against his walls, deprived of mystery and immensity, reduced to his comprehension and his size, affirmative of his assumptions, as tame and predictable as a shelf of whatnots.

Throughout their history here, most white men have moved across the North American continent following the fictive coordinates of their own self-affirming assumptions. They have followed maps, memories, dreams, plans, hopes, schemes, greeds. Seldom have they looked beyond the enclosure of preconception and desire to see where they were:

and the few who have looked beyond have seldom
been changed by what they saw. Blind to where they
were, it was inevitable that they should become the
destroyers of what was there.

John Burroughs

From "The Art of Seeing Things" in
Leaf and Tendril

I do not purpose to attempt to tell my reader how
to see things, but only to talk about the art of seeing things, as one might talk of any other art. One
might discourse about the art of poetry, or of paint-
ing, or of oratory, without any hope of making one's
readers or hearers poets or painters or orators.

The science of anything may be taught or acquired by study; the art of it comes by practice or
inspiration. The art of seeing things is not something that may be conveyed in rules and precepts;
it is a matter vital in the eye and ear, yea, in the
mind and soul, of which these are the organs. I have
as little hope of being able to tell the reader how to
see things as I would have in trying to tell him how
to fall in love or to enjoy his dinner. Either he does

or he does not, and that is about all there is of it. Some people seem born with eyes in their heads, and others with buttons or painted marbles, and no amount of science can make the one equal to the other in the art of seeing things. The great mass of mankind are, in this respect, like the rank and file of an army: they fire vaguely in the direction of the enemy, and if they hit, it is more a matter of chance than of accurate aim. But here and there is the keen-eyed observer; he is the sharpshooter; his eye selects and discriminates, his purpose goes to the mark.

Even the successful angler seems born, and not made; he appears to know instinctively the ways of trout. The secret is, no doubt, love of the sport. Love sharpens the eye, the ear, the touch; it quickens the feet, it steadies the hand, it arms against the wet and the cold. What we love to do, that we do well. To know is not all; it is only half. To love is the other half. Wordsworth's poet was contented if he might enjoy the things which others understood. This is generally the attitude of the young and of the poetic nature. The man of science, on the other hand, is contented if he may understand the things that others enjoy: that is his enjoyment. Contemplation and absorption for the one; investigation and classification for the other. We probably all have, in varying degrees, one or the other of these ways of enjoying Nature: either the sympathetic and emotional enjoyment of her which the young and the artistic and the poetic temperament have, or the enjoyment through our knowing faculties afforded by natural science, or, it may be, the two combined, as they certainly were in such a man as Tyndall.

But nothing can take the place of love. Love is the measure of life: only so far as we love do we really live. The variety of our interests, the width of our sympathies, the susceptibilities of our hearts—if these do not measure our lives, what does? As the years go by, we are all of us more or less subject to two dangers, the danger of petrifaction and the danger of putrefaction; either that we shall become hard and callous, crusted over with customs and conventions till no new ray of light or of joy can reach us, or that we shall become lax and disorganized, losing our grip upon the real and vital sources of happiness and power. Now, there is no preservative and antiseptic, nothing that keeps one's heart young, like love, like sympathy, like giving one's self with enthusiasm to some worthy thing or cause.

If I were to name the three most precious resources of life, I should say books, friends, and nature; and the greatest of these, at least the most constant and always at hand, is nature. Nature we have always with us, an inexhaustible storehouse of that which moves the heart, appeals to the mind, and fires the imagination,—health to the body, a stimulus to the intellect, and joy to the soul. To the scientist Nature is a storehouse of facts, laws, processes; to the artist she is a storehouse of pictures; to the poet she is a storehouse of images, fancies, a source of inspiration; to the moralist she is a storehouse of precepts and parables; to all she may be a source of knowledge and joy.

* * *

The book of nature is like a page written over or printed upon with different-sized characters and in many different languages, interlined and crosslined, and with a great variety of marginal notes and references. There is coarse print and fine print; there are obscure signs and hieroglyphics. We all read the large type more or less appreciatively, but only the students and lovers of nature read the fine lines and the footnotes. It is a book which he reads best who goes most slowly or even tarries long by the way. He who runs may read some things. We may take in the general features of sky, plain, and river from the express train, but only the pedestrian, the saunterer, with eyes in his head and love in his heart, turns every leaf and peruses every line. One man sees only the migrating water-fowls and the larger birds of the air; another sees the passing kinglets and hurrying warblers as well. For my part, my delight is to linger long over each page of this marvelous record, and to dwell fondly upon its most obscure text.

* * *

The eye sees what it has the means of seeing, and its means of seeing are in proportion to the love and desire behind it. The eye is informed and sharpened by the thought. My boy sees ducks on the river where and when I cannot, because at certain seasons he thinks ducks and dreams ducks. One season my neighbor asked me if the bees had injured my grapes. I said, "No; the bees never injure my grapes."

"They do mine," he replied; "they puncture the skin for the juice, and at times the clusters are covered with them."

"No," I said, "it is not the bees that puncture the skin; it is the birds."

"What birds?"

"The orioles."

"But I have n't seen any orioles," he rejoined.

"We have," I continued, "because at this season we think orioles; we have learned by experience how destructive these birds are in the vineyard, and we are on the lookout for them; our eyes and ears are ready for them."

If we think birds, we shall see birds wherever we go; if we think arrowheads, as Thoreau did, we shall pick up arrowheads in every field. Some people have an eye for four-leaved clovers; they see them as they walk hastily over the turf, for they already have them in their eyes. I once took a walk with the late Professor Eaton of Yale. He was just then specially interested in the mosses, and he found them, all kinds, everywhere. I can see him yet, every few minutes upon his knees, adjusting his eye-glasses before some rare specimen. The beauty he found in them, and pointed out to me, kindled my enthusiasm also. I once spent a summer day at the mountain home of a well-known literary woman and editor. She lamented the absence of birds about her house. I named a half-dozen or more I had heard or seen in her trees within an hour—the indigo-bird, the purple finch, the yellowbird, the veery thrush, the red-eyed vireo, the song sparrow.

"Do you mean to say you have seen or heard all these birds while sitting here on my porch?" she inquired.

"I really have," I said.

"I do not see them or hear them," she replied, "and yet I want to very much."

"No," said I; "you only *want to want* to see and hear them."

You must have the bird in your heart before you can find it in the bush.

I was sitting in front of a farmhouse one day in company with the local Nimrod. In a maple tree in front of us I saw the great crested flycatcher. I called the hunter's attention to it, and asked him if he had ever seen that bird before. No, he had not; it was a new bird to him. But he probably had seen it scores of times,—seen it without regarding it. It was not the game he was in quest of, and his eye heeded it not.

Human and artificial sounds and objects thrust themselves upon us; they are within our sphere, so to speak: but the life of nature we must meet halfway; it is shy, withdrawn, and blends itself with a vast neutral background. We must be initiated; it is an order the secrets of which are well guarded.

Annie Dillard

From "Teaching a Stone to Talk: Expeditions and
Encounters" in *Teaching a Stone to Talk*

I

The island where I live is peopled with cranks like
myself. In a cedar-shake shack on a cliff—but we
all live like this—is a man in his thirties who lives
alone with a stone he is trying to teach to talk.

Wisecracks on this topic abound, as you might
expect, but they are made as it were perfunctorily,
and mostly by the young. For in fact, almost everyone here respects what Larry is doing, as do I, which
is why I am protecting his (or her) privacy, and
confusing for you the details. It could be, for instance, a pinch of sand he is teaching to talk, or a
prolonged northerly, or any one of a number of
waves. But it is, in fact, I assure you, a stone. It is—
for I have seen it—a palm-sized oval beach cobble
whose dark gray is cut by a band of white which
runs around and, presumably, through it; such

26

stones we call "wishing stones," for reasons obscure but not, I think, unimaginable.

He keeps it on a shelf. Usually the stone lies protected by a square of untanned leather, like a canary asleep under its cloth. Larry removes the cover for the stone's lessons, or more accurately, I should say, for the ritual or rituals which they perform together several times a day.

No one knows what goes on at these sessions, least of all myself, for I know Larry but slightly, and that owing only to a mix-up in our mail. I assume that like any other meaningful effort, the ritual involves sacrifice, the suppression of self-consciousness, and a certain precise tilt of the will, so that the will becomes transparent and hollow, a channel for the work. I wish him well. It is a noble work, and beats, from any angle, selling shoes.

Reports differ on precisely what he expects or wants the stone to say. I do not think he expects the stone to speak as we do, and describe for us its long life and many, or few, sensations. I think instead that he is trying to teach it to say a single word, such as "cup," or "uncle." For this purpose he has not, as some have seriously suggested, carved the stone a little mouth, or furnished it in any way with a pocket of air which it might then expel. Rather— and I think he is wise in this—he plans to initiate his son, who is now an infant living with Larry's estranged wife, into the work, so that it may continue and bear fruit after his death.

II

Nature's silence is its one remark, and every flake of world is a chip off that old mute and immutable block. The Chinese say that we live in the world of the ten thousand things. Each of the ten thousand things cries out to us precisely nothing.

God used to rage at the Israelites for frequenting sacred groves. I wish I could find one. Martin Buber says: "The crisis of all primitive mankind comes with the discovery of that which is fundamentally not-holy, the a-sacramental, which withstands the methods, and which has no 'hour,' a province which steadily enlarges itself." Now we are no longer primitive; now the whole world seems not-holy. We have drained the light from the boughs in the sacred grove and snuffed it in the high places and along the banks of sacred streams.

We as a people have moved from pantheism to pan-atheism. Silence is not our heritage but our destiny; we live where we want to live.

The soul may ask God for anything, and never fail. You may ask God for his presence, or for wisdom, and receive each at his hands. Or you may ask God, in the words of the shopkeeper's little gag sign, that he not go away mad, but just go away. Once, in Israel, an extended family of nomads did just that. They heard God's speech and found it too loud. The wilderness generation was at Sinai; it witnessed there the thick darkness where God was: "and all the people saw the thunderings, and the lightnings, and the noise of the trumpet, and the mountain smoking." It scared them witless. Then they asked Moses to beg God, please, never speak to them directly again. "Let not God speak with us, lest we die." Moses took the message. And God, pitying their self-consciousness, agreed. He agreed not to speak to the people anymore. And he added to Moses, "Go say to them, Get into your tents again."

III

It is difficult to undo our own damage, and to re-call to our presence that which we have asked to leave. It is hard to desecrate a grove and change your mind. The very holy mountains are keeping mum. We doused the burning bush and cannot rekindle it; we are lighting matches in vain under every green tree. Did the wind use to cry, and the hills shout forth praise? Now speech has perished from among the lifeless things of earth, and living things say very little to very few. Birds may crank out sweet gibberish and monkeys howl; horses neigh and pigs say, as you recall, oink oink. But so do cobbles rumble when a wave recedes, and thunders break the air in lightning storms. I call these noises silence. It could be that wherever there is motion there is noise, as when a whale breaches and smacks the water—and wherever there is stillness there is the still small voice, God's speaking from the whirlwind, nature's old song and dance, the show we drove from town. At any rate, now it is all we can do, and among our best efforts, to try to teach a given human language, English, to chimpanzees.

In the forties an American psychologist and his

wife tried to teach a chimp actually to speak. At the end of three years the creature could pronounce, in a hoarse whisper, the words "mama," "papa," and "cup." After another three years of training she could whisper, with difficulty, still only "mama," "papa," and "cup." The more recent successes at teaching chimpanzees American Sign Language are well known. Just the other day a chimp told us, if we can believe that we truly share a vocabulary, that she had been sad in the morning. I'm sorry we asked.

What have we been doing all these centuries but trying to call God back to the mountain, or, failing that, raise a peep out of anything that isn't us? What is the difference between a cathedral and a physics lab? Are not they both saying: Hello? We spy on whales and on interstellar radio objects; we starve ourselves and pray till we're blue.

IV

I have been reading comparative cosmology. At this time most cosmologists favor the picture of the evolving universe described by Lemaître and Gamow. But I prefer a suggestion made years ago by Valéry—Paul Valéry. He set forth the notion that the universe might be "head-shaped."

The mountains are great stone bells; they clang together like nuns. Who shushed the stars? There are a thousand million galaxies easily seen in the Palomar reflector; collisions between and among them do, of course, occur. But these collisions are very long and silent slides. Billions of stars sift among each other untouched, too distant even to be moved, heedless as always, hushed. The sea pronounces something, over and over, in a hoarse whisper; I cannot quite make it out. But God knows I have tried.

At a certain point you say to the woods, to the sea, to the mountains, the world, Now I am ready. Now I will stop and be wholly attentive. You empty yourself and wait, listening. After a time you hear it: there is nothing there. There is nothing but those things only, those created objects, discrete, growing or holding, or swaying, being rained on or raining, held, flooding or ebbing, standing, or spread. You feel the world's word as a tension, a hum, a single chorused note everywhere the same. This is it: this hum is the silence. Nature does utter a peep—just this one. The birds and insects, the meadows and swamps and rivers and stones and mountains and clouds: they all do it; they all don't do it. There is a vibrancy to the silence, a suppression, as if someone were gagging the world. But you wait, you give your life's length to listening, and nothing happens. The ice rolls up, the ice rolls back, and still that single note obtains. The tension, or lack of it, is intolerable. The silence is not actually suppression; instead, it is all there is.

V

We are here to witness. There is nothing else to do with those mute materials we do not need. Until Larry teaches his stone to talk, until God changes his mind, or until the pagan gods slip back to their hilltop groves, all we can do with the whole inhuman array is watch it. We can stage our own act on the planet—build our cities on its plains, dam its rivers, plant its topsoils—but our meaningful activity scarcely covers the terrain. We do not use the songbirds, for instance. We do not eat many of them; we cannot befriend them; we cannot persuade them to eat more mosquitoes or plant fewer weed seeds. We can only witness them—whoever they are. If we were not here, they would be song-birds falling in the forest. If we were not here, material events like the passage of seasons would lack even the meager meanings we are able to muster for them. The show would play to an empty house, as do all those falling stars which fall in the day-time. That is why I take walks: to keep an eye on things. And that is why I went to the Galápagos is-lands.

All this becomes especially clear on the Galápagos islands. The Galápagos islands are just plain here—and little else. They blew up out of the ocean, some plants blew in on them, some animals drifted aboard and evolved weird forms—and there they all are, whoever they are, in full swing. You can go there and watch it happen, and try to figure it out. The Galápagos are a kind of metaphysics laboratory, almost wholly uncluttered by human culture or history. Whatever happens on those bare volcanic rocks happens in full view, whether any-one is watching or not.

What happens there is this, and precious little it is: clouds come and go, and the round of similar seasons; a pig eats a tortoise or doesn't eat a tortoise; Pacific waves fall up and slide back; a lichen expands; night follows day; an albatross dies and dries on a cliff; a cool current upwells from the ocean floor; fishes multiply, flies swarm, stars rise and fall, and diving birds dive. The news, in other words, breaks on the beaches. And taking it all in are the trees. The *palo santo* trees crowd the hillsides like any outdoor audience; they face the lagoons, the lava lowlands, and the shores.

I have some experience of these *palo santo* trees. They interest me as emblems of the muteness of the human stance in relation to all that is not human. I see us all as *palo santo* trees, holy sticks, together watching all that we watch, and growing in silence.

In the Galápagos , it took me a long time to notice the *palo santo* trees. Like everyone else, I specialized in sea lions. My shipmates and I liked the sea lions, and envied their lives. Their joy seemed conscious. They were engaged in full-time play. They were all either fat or dead; there was no halfway. By day they played in the shallows, alone or together, greeting each other and us with great noises of joy, or they took a turn offshore and body-surfed in the breakers, exultant. By night on the sand they lay in each other's flippers and slept. Everyone joked, often, that when he "came back," he would just as soon do it all over again as a sea lion. I concurred. The sea lion game looked un-beatable.

But a year and a half later, I returned to those unpeopled islands. In the interval my attachment to them had shifted, and my memories of them had altered, the way memories do, like particolored pebbles rolled back and forth over a grating, so that after a time those hard bright ones, the ones you thought you would never lose, have vanished, passed through the grating, and only a few big, unexpected ones remain, no longer unnoticed but now selected out for some meaning, large and un-known.

Such were the *palo santo* trees. Before, I had never given them a thought. They were just miles of half-dead trees on the red lava sea cliffs of some deserted islands. They were only a name in a note-book: "*palo santo*—those strange white trees." Look at the sea lions! Look at the flightless cormorants, the penguins, the iguanas, the sunset! But after eighteen months the wonderful cormorants, penguins, iguanas, sunsets, and even the sea lions, had dropped from my holey heart. I returned to the Galápagos to see the *palo santo* trees.

They are thin, pale, wispy trees. You walk among them on the lowland deserts, where they grow beside the prickly pear. You see them from the water on the steeps that face the sea, hundreds together, small and thin and spread, and so much more pale than their red soils that any black-and-white photograph of them looks like a negative. Their stands look like blasted orchards. At every season they all look newly dead, pale and bare as birches drowned in a beaver pond—for at every season they look leafless, paralyzed, and mute. But in fact, if you look closely, you can see during the rainy months a few meager deciduous leaves here and there on their brittle twigs. And hundreds of lichens always grow on their bark in mute, overlapping explosions which barely enlarge in the course of the decade, lichens pink and orange, lavender, yellow, and green. The *palo santo* trees bear the lichens effortlessly, unconsciously, the way they bear everything.

Their multitudes, transparent as line drawings, crowd the cliffsides like whirling dancers, like empty groves, and look out over cliff-wrecked breakers toward more unpeopled islands, with their freakish lizards and birds, toward the grieving lagoons and the bays where the sea lions wander, and beyond to the clamoring seas.

Now I no longer concurred with my shipmates' joke; I no longer wanted to "come back" as a sea lion. For I thought, and I still think, that if I came back to life in the sunlight where everything changes, I would like to come back as a *palo santo* tree, one of thousands on a cliffside on those godforsaken islands, where a million events occur among the witless, where a splash of rain may drop on a yellow iguana the size of a dachshund, and ten minutes later the iguana may blink. I would like to come back as a *palo santo* tree on the weather side of an island, so that I could be, myself, a perfect witness, and look, mute, and wave my arms.

VI

The silence is all there is. It is the alpha and the omega. It is God's brooding over the face of the waters; it is the blended note of the ten thousand things, the whine of wings. You take a step in the right direction to pray to this silence, and even to address the prayer to "World." Distinctions blur. Quit your tents. Pray without ceasing.

Gretel Ehrlich

"Looking for a Lost Dog" in
Islands, The Universe, Home

The most valuable thoughts which I entertain are
anything but what I thought. Nature abhors a
vacuum, and if I can only walk with sufficient care-
lessness I am sure to be filled.

THOREAU

I started off this morning looking for a lost dog.
He's a red heeler, blotched brown and white, and I
tell people he looks like a big saddle shoe. Born at
Christmas on a thirty-below-zero night, he's tough,
though his right front leg is crooked where it froze
to the ground.

It's the old needle-in-the-haystack routine: small
dog—huge landscape and rugged terrain. I go one

way, my husband the other. I walk and I listen. While moving cows once, the dog fell in a hole and disappeared. We heard him whining but couldn't see where he had gone. I crouched down, put my ear to the ground, and crawled toward the whines.

It's no wonder human beings are so narcissistic. The way our ears are constructed, we can hear only what is right next to us or else the internal monologue inside. I've taken to cupping my hands behind my ears—mulelike—and pricking them all the way forward or back to hear what's happened or what's ahead.

"Life is polyphonic," a Hungarian friend in her eighties said. She was a child prodigy from Budapest who had soloed on the violin in Paris and Berlin by the time she was twelve. "Childishly, I once thought hearing had mostly to do with music. Now that I'm too old to play the fiddle, I know it has to do with the great suspiration of life everywhere."

But back to the dog. I'm walking and looking and listening for him, though there is no trail, no clue, no direction to the search. Whimsically, I head north toward the falls. They're set in a deep gorge where Precambrian rock piles up to ten thousand feet on either side. A raven creaks overhead, flies into the cleft, glides toward a panel of white water splashing over a ledge, and comes out cawing.

To find what is lost is an art in some cultures. The Navajos employ "hand tremblers"—usually women—who go into a trance and "see" where the lost article or person is located. When I asked one such diviner what it was like when she was in trance, she said, "Lots of noise but noise that's hard to hear."

Near the falls the ground flattens out into a high-altitude valley before the mountain rises vertically. The falls roar, but they are overgrown with spruce, pine, and willow, and the closer I get, the harder it is to see them. Perhaps that is how it will be in my search for the dog.

We're worried about Frenchy, because last summer he was bitten three times by rattlesnakes. After the first bite he walked toward me, reeled, and collapsed. His eyes rolled back, and he drooled. I could see the two holes where the fangs went in. They looked like little eyes spying on me. I was sure the dog was dying. He lay in my arms for a long time, while I crooned to him. My last rites, however, seemed to have had the opposite effect: he perked up suddenly, then gave me a funny look as if to say, "Shut up, you fool." I drove him twenty miles to the vet's house. By the time we arrived, he resembled a monster. His nose and neck had swollen as though a football had been sewn under the skin.

I walk and walk. Past the falls, through a pass, toward a larger, rowdier creek. The sky goes black. In the distance, snow on the Owl Creek Mountains glares. A blue ocean seems to stretch between, and the black sky hangs over like a frown.

A string of cottonwoods whose tender leaves are the color of limes pulls me downstream. I come to the meadow with the abandoned apple orchard. Its trees have lost most of their blossoms; I feel as if I had caught them undressed.

The sun comes back, and the wind. It brings no dog, but ducks slide overhead. An Eskimo from Barrow told me the reason spring has such fierce winds is so the birds coming north will have something to fly on.

To find what is lost; to lose what is found. Several times I've thought I was losing my mind. Of course, minds aren't literally misplaced; on the contrary, we live too much in them. We listen gullibly, then feel severed because of the mind's clever tyrannies. As with viewing the falls, we can lose sight of what is too close, and the struggle between impulse and reason, passion and logic, occurs as we saunter from distant to close-up views.

The feet move; the mind wanders. In his essay on walking, Thoreau said, "The saunterer, in the good sense, is no more vagrant than the meandering river, which is all the while sedulously seeking the shortest course to the sea."

Today I'm filled with longings—for what I'm not, for all the other lives I can't lead, for what is impossible, for people I love who can't be in my life. Passions of all sorts struggle soundlessly, or else, like the falls, they are all noise but can't be seen.

Now I'm following a game trail up a sidehill. It's a mosaic of tracks—elk and deer, rabbit and bird. If city dwellers could imprint cement as they walked, it would look this way: tracks overlap, go backward and forward like the peregrine saunterings of the mind.

I see a dog track, or is it a coyote's? I get down on my hands and knees to sniff out a scent. What am I doing? I entertain preposterous expectations of myself as when I landed in Tokyo, where I felt so at home I thought I would break into fluent Japanese. Now I sniff the ground and smell only dirt. If I tried and tried, would the instinct regenerate inside me?

The tracks veer off the trail and disappear. Descending into a dry wash whose elegant tortured junipers resemble bonsai, I trip on a sagebrush root, and look. Deep in the center, there is a bird's nest. Instead of eggs, a locust stares up at me.

Some days I think this one place isn't enough. That's when nothing is enough, when I want to live multiple lives and have the know-how and guts to love without limits. Those days, like today, I walk with a purpose but no destination. Only then do I see, at least momentarily, that most everything is here. To my left a towering cottonwood is lunatic with bird song. Under it, I'm a listening post while its great, gray trunk—like a baton—heaves its green symphony into the air.

I walk and walk, from the falls, over Grouse Hill, to the dry wash. Today it is enough to make a shadow.

Charles Kuralt

"Angler" in

On the Road with Charles Kuralt

Upper Peninsula, Michigan

Judge John Voelker, Michigan Supreme Court, re-
tired. In the wintertime he writes books. He wrote
Anatomy of a Murder among others. In the spring
and summer, every day of the trout season, he fishes
for trout. John Voelker is an uncommon man, a
man, you might even say, who is in revolt. It is bigness he is revolting against, the old and widely ac-
cepted idea of the bigger the better. John Voelker
fishes only with the tiniest flies, tied to gossamer
leaders, and fishes only for the smallest fish, the
beautiful native brook trout which inhabit the
ponds and streams of his beloved Upper Peninsula
of Michigan. They are elusive circles in the water,
but knowing they're there is enough for John

Voelker, alone in the backwoods, a long way from the big buildings of the big cities of this big country.

*   *   *

Voelker: Hey, a little one! Here is a tiny fish, maybe not big enough to keep legally, and I'm not going to keep him. I mean, imagine going out in a boat winching in fish. I guess there's a thrill in it, a lot of people do it. While it keeps a lot of pressure from this water, for which I'm thankful, there's a kind of a sadness in it. It's part of this bigness thing. And a ten-inch trout here on this tackle is like catching a five-pound rainbow. In fact, in a way, it's a little more difficult. Some of these guys use hawsers, you know; you could tow a tugboat with some of the gear that they use. [Puts fish back] He's going to make it. His feelings are hurt, but he'll make it.

Why do you do it? I asked him. Why do you spend every day fishing? "Well," he said, "I wrote it down once. I'll go find it and say it for you if you'd like." He did and we were glad he did.

Voelker: I fish because I love to. Because I love the environs where trout are found, which are invariably beautiful, and hate the environs where crowds of people are found, which are invariably ugly. Because of all the television commercials, cocktail parties and assorted social posturing I thus escape. Because in a world where most men seem to spend their lives doing what they hate, my fishing is at once an endless source of delight and an act of small rebellion. Because trout do not lie or cheat and cannot be bought or bribed, or impressed by power, but respond only to quietude and humility, and endless patience. Because I suspect that men are going along this way for the last time and I for one don't want to waste the trip. Because mercifully there are no telephones on trout waters. Because only in the woods can I find solitude without loneliness. Because bourbon out of an old tin cup always tastes better out there. Because maybe one day I will catch a mermaid. And finally, not because I regard fishing as being so terribly important, but because I suspect that so many of the other concerns of men are equally unimportant and not nearly so much fun. Amen

Aldo Leopold

"March" in

A Sand County Almanac: And Sketches Here and There

The Geese Return

One swallow does not make a summer, but one skein of geese, cleaving the murk of a March thaw, is the spring.

A cardinal, whistling spring to a thaw but later finding himself mistaken, can retrieve his error by resuming his winter silence. A chipmunk, emerging for a sunbath but finding a blizzard, has only to go back to bed. But a migrating goose, staking two hundred miles of black night on the chance of finding a hole in the lake, has no easy chance for retreat. His arrival carries the conviction of a prophet who has burned his bridges.

A March morning is only as drab as he who walks in it without a glance skyward, ear cocked for geese. I once knew an educated lady, banded by

Phi Beta Kappa, who told me that she had never
heard or seen the geese that twice a year proclaim
the revolving seasons to her well-insulated roof. Is
education possibly a process of trading awareness
for things of lesser worth? The goose who trades
his is soon a pile of feathers.

The geese that proclaim the seasons to our farm
are aware of many things, including the Wisconsin
statutes. The southbound November flocks pass
over us high and haughty, with scarcely a honk of
recognition for their favorite sandbars and sloughs.
'As a crow flies' is crooked compared with their
undeviating aim at the nearest big lake twenty miles
to the south, where they loaf by day on broad waters and filch corn by night from the freshly cut
stubbles. November geese are aware that every
marsh and pond bristles from dawn till dark with
hopeful guns.

March geese are a different story. Although they
have been shot at most of the winter, as attested by
their buckshot-battered pinions, they know that the
spring truce is now in effect. They wind the ox-
bows of the river, cutting low over the now gunless
points and islands, and gabbling to each sandbar

as to a long-lost friend. They weave low over the marshes and meadows, greeting each newly melted puddle and pool. Finally, after a few *pro-forma* circlings of our marsh, they set wing and glide silently to the pond, black landing-gear lowered and rumps white against the far hill. Once touching water, our newly arrived guests set up a honking and splashing that shakes the last thought of winter out of the brittle cattails. Our geese are home again!

It is at this moment of each year that I wish I were a muskrat, eye-deep in the marsh.

Once the first geese are in, they honk a clamorous invitation to each migrating flock, and in a few days the marsh is full of them. On our farm we measure the amplitude of our spring by two yardsticks: the number of pines planted, and the number of geese that stop. Our record is 642 geese counted in on 11 April 1946.

As in fall, our spring geese make daily trips to corn, but these are no surreptitious sneakings-out by night; the flocks move noisily to and from corn stubbles through the day. Each departure is preceded by loud gustatory debate, and each return by an even louder one. The returning flocks, once thoroughly at home, omit their *pro-forma* circlings of the marsh. They tumble out of the sky like maple leaves, side-slipping right and left to lose altitude, feet spraddled toward the shouts of welcome below. I suppose the ensuing gabble deals with the merits of the day's dinner. They are now eating the waste corn that the snow blanket has protected over winter from corn-seeking crows, cottontails, meadow mice, and pheasants.

It is a conspicuous fact that the corn stubbles selected by geese for feeding are usually those occupying former prairies. No man knows whether this bias for prairie corn reflects some superior nutritional value, or some ancestral tradition transmitted from generation to generation since the prairie days. Perhaps it reflects the simpler fact that prairie cornfields tend to be large. If I could understand the thunderous debates that precede and follow these daily excursions to corn, I might soon learn the reason for the prairie-bias. But I cannot, and I am well content that it should remain a mystery. What a dull world if we knew all about geese!

In thus watching the daily routine of a spring

goose convention, one notices the prevalence of singles—lone geese that do much flying about and much talking. One is apt to impute a disconsolate tone to their honkings, and to jump to the conclusion that they are broken-hearted widowers, or mothers hunting lost children. The seasoned ornithologist knows, however, that such subjective interpretation of bird behavior is risky. I long tried to keep an open mind on the question.

After my students and I had counted for half a dozen years the number of geese comprising a flock, some unexpected light was cast on the meaning of lone geese. It was found by mathematical analysis that flocks of six or multiples of six were far more frequent than chance alone would dictate. In other words, goose flocks are families, or aggregations of families, and lone geese in spring are probably just what our fond imaginings had first suggested. They are bereaved survivors of the winter's shooting, searching in vain for their kin. Now I am free to grieve with and for the lone honkers.

It is not often that cold-potato mathematics thus confirms the sentimental promptings of the bird-lover.

On April nights when it has become warm
enough to sit outdoors, we love to listen to the pro-
ceedings of the convention in the marsh. There are
long periods of silence when one hears only the
winnowing of snipe, the hoot of a distant owl, or
the nasal clucking of some amorous coot. Then, of
a sudden, a strident honk resounds, and in an instant pandemonium echoes. There is a beating of
pinions on water, a rushing of dark prows propelled
by churning paddles, and a general shouting by the
onlookers of a vehement controversy. Finally some
deep honker has his last word, and the noise sub-
sides to that half-audible small-talk that seldom
ceases among geese. Once again, I would I were a
muskrat!

By the time the pasques are in full bloom our
goose-convention dwindles, and before May our
marsh is once again a mere grassy wetness, enliv-
ened only by redwings and rails.

*   *   *

It is an irony of history that the great powers should
have discovered the unity of nations at Cairo in

1943. The geese of the world have had that notion for a longer time, and each March they stake their lives on its essential truth.

In the beginning there was only the unity of the Ice Sheet. Then followed the unity of the March thaw, and the northward hegira of the international geese. Every March since the Pleistocene, the geese have honked unity from China Sea to Siberian Steppe, from Euphrates to Volga, from Nile to Murmansk, from Lincolnshire to Spitsbergen. Every March since the Pleistocene, the geese have honked unity from Currituck to Labrador, Matamuskeet to Ungava, Horseshoe Lake to Hudson's Bay, Avery Island to Baffin Land, Panhandle to Mackenzie, Sacramento to Yukon.

By this international commerce of geese, the waste corn of Illinois is carried through the clouds to the Arctic tundras, there to combine with the waste sunlight of a nightless June to grow goslings for all the lands between. And in this annual barter of food for light, and winter warmth for summer solitude, the whole continent receives as net profit a wild poem dropped from the murky skies upon the muds of March.

Barry Holstun Lopez

"The Bend" in
River Notes: The Dance of Herons

In the evenings I walk down and stand in the trees, in light paused just so in the leaves, as if the change in the river here were not simply known to me but apprehended. It did not start out this way; I began with the worst sort of ignorance, the grossest inquiries. Now I ask very little. I observe the swift movement of water through the nation of fish at my feet. I wonder privately if there are for them, as there are for me, moments of faith.

The river comes around from the southeast to the east at this point: a clean shift of direction, water deep and fast on the outside of the curve, flowing slower over the lip of a broad gravel bar on the inside, continuing into a field of shattered boulders to the west.

I kneel and slip my hands like frogs beneath the surface of the water. I feel the wearing away of the outer edge, the exposure of rootlets, the undermining. I imagine eyes in the tips of my fingers, like the eyestalks of crayfish. Fish stare at my fingertips and bolt into the river's darkness. I withdraw my hands, conscious of the trespass. The thought that I might be observed disturbs me.

I've wanted to take the measure of this turn in the river, grasp it for private reasons. I feel closer to it now. I know which deer drink at which spots on this bank. I know of the small screech owl nesting opposite (I would point him out to you by throwing a stone in that direction but the gesture would not be appropriate). I am familiar with the raccoon and fisher whose tracks appear here, can even tell them apart in the dark by delicately fingering the rim of their prints in the soil. I can hear the preparations of muskrats. On cold, damp nights I am aware of the fog of birds' breath that rolls oceanic through the trees above. Out there, I know which rocks are gripped by slumbering water striders, and where beneath the water lie the slipcase homes of caddis fly larvae.

I feel I am coming closer to it.

For myself, each day more of me slips away. Absorbed in seeing how the water comes through the bend, just so, I am myself, sliding off.

The attempt to wrestle meaning from this spot began poorly, with illness. A pain, slow in coming like so many, that seemed centered in the back of my neck. Then an acute yearning, as strong as the wish to be loved, pain along the ribs, and my legs started to give way. I awoke in the morning with my hands over my face as though astonished by my own dreams. As the weeks went on I moved about less and less, until finally I went to bed and lay there like summer leaves. I could hear the rain in the woods in the afternoon; the sound of the river, like the laughing of horses; smell faintly through the open window the breath of bears. Between these points I was contained, closed off like a spider by the design of a web. I tried to imagine that I was well, but the points of my imagination impaled me, and then a sense of betrayal emptied me.

I began to think (as on a staircase descending to an unexamined basement) about the turn in the river. If I could understand this smoothly done change of direction I could imitate it, I reasoned, just as a man puts what he reads in a story to use, substituting one point for another as he needs.

Several things might be measured I speculated: the rate of flow of the water, the erosion of the outer bank, the slope of the adjacent mountains, the changing radius of curvature as the river turned west. It could be revealed neatly, affirmed with graphic authority.

I became obsessed with its calculation. I lay the plan out first in my head, without recourse to paper. The curve required calculus, and so some loss of accuracy; and the precise depth of the river changed from moment to moment, as did its width. But I could abide this for the promise of insight into my life.

I called on surveyors, geodesic scientists, hydrologists. It was the work of half a year. It involved them in the arduous toting of instruments back and forth across the river and in tedious calculation. I asked that exacting journals be kept, that no scrap of description be lost. There were arguments, of course. I required that renderings be done again, over and over. I became convinced that in this wealth of detail a fixed reason for the river's graceful turn would inevitably be revealed.

The workmen, defeated by the precision required, in an anger all their own, hurled their theodolites into the trees. (The repair of these instruments consumed more time.) I understood that fights broke out. But I saw none of this. I lay alone in the room and those in my employ came and went politely with their notes. I knew they thought it pointless, but there was their own employment to be considered, and they said the wage was fair.

Finally they reduced the bend in the river to an elegant series of equations, and the books containing them and a bewildering list of variables were all gathered together and brought to my room. I had them placed on the floor, stacked in a corner. I suddenly had the strength for the first time, staring at this pile, to move, but I was afraid. I put it off until morning; I felt my recovery was certain, believed even more forcefully now that my own resolution was at hand by an incontestable analogy.

That night I awoke to hear the dripping of water. From the direction of the pile of notes came the sound of mergansers, the explosive sound they make when they are surprised on the water and suddenly fly off.

I lay back.

Moss grew eventually on the books. They began after a while to harden, to resemble the gray boulders in the river. Years passed. I smelled cottonwood on spring afternoons, and would imagine sunshine crinkling on the surface of the water.

In winter the windows remained open because I could not reach them.

One morning, without warning, I came to a dead space in my depression, a sudden horizontal view, which I seized. I pried myself from the room, coming down the stairs slow step by slow step, all the while calling out. Bears heard me (or were already waiting at the door). I told them I needed to be near the river. They carried me through the trees (growling, for they are not used to working together), throwing their shoulders to the alders until we stood at the outer bank.

Then they departed, leaving the odor of bruised grass and cracked bone hanging in the air.

The first thing I did was to feel, raccoonlike, with

the tips of my fingers the soil of the bank just below the water's edge. I listened for the sound of
water on the outer bar. I observed the hunt of the
caddis fly.

I am now taking the measure of the bend in these
experiences.

I have lost, as I have said, some sense of myself.
I no longer require as much. And though I am hopeful of recovery, an adjustment as smooth as the way
the river lies against the earth at this point, this is
no longer the issue with me. I am more interested
in this: from above, to a hawk, the bend must appear only natural and I for the moment insepara-
bly a part, like salmon or a flower. I cannot say well
enough how this single perception has dismantled
my loneliness.

John Muir

From "The River Floods" in
The Mountains of California

The storm was in full bloom, and formed, from my commanding outlook on the hilltop, one of the most glorious views I ever beheld. As far as the eye could reach, above, beneath, around, wind-driven rain filled the air like one vast waterfall. Detached clouds swept imposingly up the valley, as if they were endowed with independent motion and had special work to do in replenishing the mountain wells, now rising above the pine-tops, now descending into their midst, fondling their arrowy spires and soothing every branch and leaf with gentleness in the midst of all the savage sound and motion. Others keeping near the ground glided behind separate groves, and brought them forward into relief with admirable distinctness; or, passing in front, eclipsed whole groves in succession, pine after pine melting in their gray fringes and bursting forth again seemingly clearer than before.

The forms of storms are in great part measured, and controlled by the topography of the regions where they rise and over which they pass. When, therefore, we attempt to study them from the valleys, or from gaps and openings of the forest, we are confounded by a multitude of separate and apparently antagonistic impressions. The bottom of the storm is broken up into innumerable waves and currents that surge against the hillsides like sea-waves against a shore, and these, reacting on the nether surface of the storm, erode immense cavernous hollows and cañons, and sweep forward the resulting detritus in long trains, like the moraines of glaciers. But, as we ascend, these partial, confusing effects disappear and the phenomena are beheld united and harmonious.

The longer I gazed into the storm, the more plainly visible it became. The drifting cloud detritus gave it a kind of visible body, which explained many perplexing phenomena, and published its movements in plain terms, while the texture of the falling mass of rain rounded it out and rendered it more complete. Because raindrops differ in size they fall at different velocities and overtake and clash against one another, producing mist and spray. They also, of course, yield unequal compliance to the force of the wind, which gives rise to a still greater degree of interference, and passionate gusts sweep off clouds of spray from the groves like that torn from wave-tops in a gale. All these factors of irregularity in density, color, and texture of the general rain mass tend to make it the more appreciable and telling. It is then seen as one grand flood rushing over bank and brae, bending the pines like weeds, curving this way and that, whirling in huge eddies in hollows and dells, while the main current pours grandly over all, like ocean currents over the landscapes that lie hidden at the bottom of the sea.

I watched the gestures of the pines while the storm was at its height, and it was easy to see that they were not distressed. Several large Sugar Pines stood near the thicket in which I was sheltered, bowing solemnly and tossing their long arms as if interpreting the very words of the storm while accepting its wildest onsets with passionate exhilaration. The lions were feeding. Those who have observed sunflowers feasting on sunshine during the golden days of Indian summer know that none of their gestures express thankfulness. Their celestial food is too heartily given, too heartily taken to leave room for thanks. The pines were evidently accepting the benefactions of the storm in the same whole-souled manner; and when I looked down among the budding hazels, and still lower to the young violets and fern-tufts on the rocks, I noticed the same divine methods of giving and taking, and the same exquisite adaptations of what seems an outbreak of violent and uncontrollable force to the purposes of beautiful and delicate life. Calms like sleep come upon landscapes, just as they do on people and trees, and storms awaken them in the same way. In the dry midsummer of the lower portion of the range the withered hills and valleys seem to lie as empty and expressionless as dead shells on a shore. Even the highest mountains may be found occasionally dull and uncommunicative as if in some way they had lost countenance and shrunk to less than half their real stature. But when the lightings crash and echo in the cañons, and the clouds come down wreathing and crowning their bald snowy heads, every feature beams with expression and they rise again in all their imposing majesty.

Storms are fine speakers, and tell all they know, but their voices of lightning, torrent, and rushing wind are much less numerous than the nameless still, small voices too low for human ears; and because we are poor listeners we fail to catch much that is fairly within reach. Our best rains are heard mostly on roofs, and winds in chimneys; and when by choice or compulsion we are pushed into the heart of a storm, the confusion made by cumbersome equipments and nervous haste and mean fear, prevent our hearing any other than the loudest expressions. Yet we may draw enjoyment from storm sounds that are beyond hearing, and storm movements we cannot see. The sublime whirl of planets around their suns is as silent as raindrops oozing in the dark among the roots of plants. In this great storm, as in every other, there were tones and gestures inexpressibly gentle manifested in the midst of what is called violence and fury, but easily recognized by all who look and listen for them. The

rain brought out the colors of the woods with delightful freshness, the rich brown of the bark of the
trees and the fallen burs and leaves and dead ferns;
the grays of rocks and lichens; the light purple of
swelling buds, and the warm yellow greens of the
libocedrus and mosses. The air was steaming with
delightful fragrance, not rising and wafting past in
separate masses, but diffused through all the atmosphere. Pine woods are always fragrant, but most
so in spring when the young tassels are opening
and in warm weather when the various gums and
balsams are softened by the sun. The wind was now
chafing their innumerable needles and the warm
rain was steeping them. Monardella grows here in
large beds in the openings, and there is plenty of
laurel in dells and manzanita on the hillsides, and
the rosy, fragrant chamœbatia carpets the ground
almost everywhere. These, with the gums and balsams of the woods, form the main local fragrance-
fountains of the storm. The ascending clouds of
aroma wind-rolled and rain-washed became pure
like light and traveled with the wind as part of it.
Toward the middle of the afternoon the main flood
cloud lifted along its western border revealing a

beautiful section of the Sacramento Valley some twenty or thirty miles away, brilliantly sun-lighted and glistering with rain-sheets as if paved with silver. Soon afterward a jagged bluff-like cloud with a sheer face appeared over the valley of the Yuba, dark-colored and roughened with numerous furrows like some huge lava-table. The blue Coast Range was seen stretching along the sky like a beveled wall, and the somber, craggy Marysville Buttes rose impressively out of the flooded plain like islands out of the sea. Then the rain began to abate and I sauntered down through the dripping bushes reveling in the universal vigor and freshness that inspired all the life about me. How clean and unworn and immortal the woods seemed to be!—the lofty cedars in full bloom laden with golden pollen and their washed plumes shining; the pines rocking gently and settling back into rest, and the evening sunbeams spangling on the broad leaves of the madroños, their tracery of yellow boughs relieved against dusky thickets of Chestnut Oak; liverworts, lycopodiums, ferns were exulting in glorious revival, and every moss that had ever lived seemed to be coming crowding back from the dead to clothe each trunk and stone in living green. The steaming ground seemed fairly to throb and tingle with life; smilax, fritillaria, saxifrage, and young violets were pushing up as if already conscious of the summer glory, and innumerable green and yellow buds were peeping and smiling everywhere.

As for the birds and squirrels, not a wing or tail of them was to be seen while the storm was blowing. Squirrels dislike wet weather more than cats do; therefore they were at home rocking in their dry nests. The birds were hiding in the dells out of the wind, some of the strongest of them pecking at acorns and manzanita berries, but most were perched on low twigs, their breast feathers puffed out and keeping one another company through the hard time as best they could.

When I arrived at the village about sundown, the good people bestirred themselves, pitying my bedraggled condition as if I were some benumbed castaway snatched from the sea, while I, in turn, warm with excitement and reeking like the ground, pitied them for being dry and defrauded of all the glory that Nature had spread round about them that day.

Luther Standing Bear

From "Hunter, Scout, Warrior" in
Land of the Spotted Eagle

It is said that Nature makes the man to fit his surroundings. If that be the case, then a description of
the land partly, at least, describes the people. Our
homeland was proportioned on a big scale. There
seemed to be nothing small, nothing limited, in our
domain. Our home, which covered part of North
Dakota, all of South Dakota, and part of Nebraska
and Wyoming, was one of great plains, large rivers
and wooded mountains. So wide were the prairies
that the sun seemed to rise out of one distant edge
and in the evening to set in the opposite distant
edge. The weather was extreme. The winter was cold
with sleet and ice and the temperature often below
zero. The winds were so strong they made us feel
their strength. The summers were hot and violent

with color. At times the skies were as blue as Lakota blue paint and as far as the eye could see the earth was a deep green, while the sun set in red as dazzling to the eye as the white of midday. The rain fell in streams and the storm warriors threw their lightning sticks to earth and shook our tipis with their thunder. We grew used to strength, height, distance, power.

Nature dealt vigorously with the Lakota and they with bodies almost bare became vigorous. What the body was fitted for the mind was fitted for also, and physical hardihood was matched with spiritual hardihood. There was little fear within. The mental reaction of the Lakota was one of unity with these tremendous forces, and rather than terror many times the attitude was a welcoming defiance. I have seen a brave, without uttering a word, strip himself to breechclout and walk out into a rain falling so heavily in sheets that a few paces from the door his form was lost to sight. He went out to be alone with Rain. That is true love of Nature.

Surroundings were filled with comforts for the body and beauty for expectant senses. Every morning the sun was received by each individual in a moment of silent reverence; and in the evening the sunset was watched, for it held the secret of the next day's weather. The springs and trees inspired songs and stories which we wrote in our minds and framed in our consciousness.

Of all our domain we loved, perhaps, the Black Hills the most. The Lakota had named these hills *He Sapa*, or Black Hills, on account of their color. The slopes and peaks were so heavily wooded with dark pines that from a distance the mountains actually looked black. In wooded recesses were numberless springs of pure water and numerous small lakes. There were wood and game in abundance and shelter from the storms of the plains. It was the favorite winter haunt of the buffalo and the Lakota as well. According to a tribal legend these hills were a reclining female figure from whose breasts flowed life-giving forces, and to them the Lakota went as a child to its mother's arms. The various entrances to the hills were very rough and rugged, but there was one very beautiful and easy pass through which both buffalo and Lakota entered the hills. This pass ran along a narrow stream bed which widened here and there but which in places narrowed so that the tall pines at the top of the cliffs arched their boughs, almost touching as they swayed in the wind. Every fall thousands of buffaloes and Lakotas went through this pass to spend the winter in the hills. *Pte ta tiyopa* it was called by the Lakotas, or 'Gate of the buffalo.' Today this beautiful pass is denuded of trees and to the white man it is merely 'Buffalo Gap.'

Two lovely legends of the Lakotas would be fine subjects for sculpturing — the Black Hills as the earth mother, and the story of the genesis of the tribe. Instead, the face of a white man is being outlined on the face of a stone cliff in the Black Hills. This beautiful region, of which the Lakota thought more than any other spot on earth, caused him the most pain and misery. These hills were to become prized by the white people for reasons far different from those of the Lakota. To the Lakota the magnificent forests and splendid herds were incomparable in value. To the white man everything was valueless except the gold in the hills. Toward the Indian the white people were absolutely devoid of sentiment, and when a people lack sentiment they are without compassion. So down went the Black

Forest and to death went the last buffalo, noble animal and immemorial friend of the Lakota. As for the people who were as native to the soil as the forests and the buffalo—well, the gold-seekers did not understand them and never have. The white man will never know the horror and the utter bewilderment of the Lakota at the wanton destruction of the buffalo. What cruelty has not been glossed over with the white man's word—enterprise! If the Lakotas had been relinquishing any part of their territory voluntarily, the Black Hills would have been the last from the standpoint of traditional sentiment. So when by false treaties and trickery the Black Hills were forever lost, they were a broken people. The treaties, made supposedly to recompense them for the loss of this lovely region, were like all other treaties—worthless. But could the Lakota braves have foreseen the ignominy they were destined to endure, every man would have died fighting rather than give up his homeland to live in subjection and helplessness.

How long the Lakota people lived in these midwest plains bordering the Black Hills before the coming of the white men is not known in tribal

records. But our legends tell us that it was hundreds
and perhaps thousands of years ago since the first
man sprang from the soil in the midst of these great
plains. The story says that one morning long ago a
lone man awoke, face to the sun, emerging from
the soil. Only his head was visible, the rest of his
body not yet being fashioned. The man looked
about, but saw no mountains, no rivers, no forests.
There was nothing but soft and quaking mud, for
the earth itself was still young. Up and up the man
drew himself until he freed his body from the cling-
ing soil. At last he stood upon the earth, but it was
not solid, and his first few steps were slow and halt-
ing. But the sun shone and ever the man kept his
face turned toward it. In time the rays of the sun
hardened the face of the earth and strengthened
the man and he bounded and leaped about, a free
and joyous creature. From this man sprang the
Lakota nation and, so far as we know, our people
have been born and have died on this plain; and no
people have shared it with us until the coming of
the European. So this land of the great plains is
claimed by the Lakotas as their very own. We are of
the soil and the soil is of us. We love the birds and

beasts that grew with us on this soil. They drank the same water we did and breathed the same air. We are all one in nature. Believing so, there was in our hearts a great peace and a welling kindness for all living, growing things.

Wallace Stegner

From "Thoughts in a Dry Land" in *Where the Bluebird Sings to the Lemonade Springs: Living and Writing in the West*

Years ago I picked up an Iowa aunt of mine in Salt Lake City and drove her down to our cottage on Fish Lake. She was not looking as we drove—she was talking—and she missed the Wasatch, and Mount Nebo, and the Sanpete Valley, and even Sigurd Mountain—the Pahvant—which some people down there call the Big Rock Candy Mountain and which is about as colorful as a peppermint stick. The first thing she really saw, as we turned east at Sigurd, was the towering, level front of the Sevier Plateau above Richfield—level as a rooftree, steep as a cliff, and surging more than a mile straight up above that lush valley. I saw it hit her, and I heard it too, for the talk stopped. I said,

"How do you like that, Aunt Min?" for like any Westerner I like to impress Iowans, and the easiest way to do it is with size. She blinked and ruffled up her feathers and assembled herself after the moment of confusion and said, "That's nice. It reminds me of the river bluffs in the county park at Fort Dodge."

She couldn't even see it. She had no experience, no scale, by which to judge an unbroken mountain wall more than a mile high, and her startled mental circuitry could respond with nothing better than the fifty-foot clay banks that her mind had learned to call scenery. She was like the soldiers of Cárdenas, the first white men who ever looked into the Grand Canyon. The river that the Indians had said was half a league wide they judged was about six feet, until they climbed a third of the way down and found that rocks the size of a man grew into things taller than the great tower of Seville, and the six-foot creek, even from four thousand feet above it, was clearly a mighty torrent.

Scale is the first and easiest of the West's lessons. Colors and forms are harder. Easterners are constantly being surprised and somehow offended that California's summer hills are gold, not green. We are creatures shaped by our experiences; we like what we know, more often than we know what we like. To eyes trained on universal chlorophyll, gold or brown hills may look repulsive. Sagebrush is an acquired taste, as are raw earth and alkali flats. The erosional forms of the dry country strike the attention without ringing the bells of appreciation. It is almost pathetic to read the journals of people who came west up the Platte Valley in the 1840s and 1850s and tried to find words for Chimney Rock and Scott's Bluff, and found and clung for dear life to the clichés of castles and silent sentinels.

Listen to Clarence Dutton on the canyon country, whose forms and colors are as far from Hudson River School standards as any in the West:

The lover of nature, whose perceptions have been trained in the Alps, in Italy, Germany, or New England, in the Appalachians or Cordilleras, in Scotland or Colorado, would enter this strange region with a shock, and dwell there for a time with a sense of oppression, and perhaps with horror. Whatsoever things he had learned to regard as beautiful and noble he would seldom or never see, and whatsoever he might see would appear to him as anything but beautiful and noble. Whatsoever might be bold and striking would at first seem only grotesque. The colors would be the very ones he had learned to shun as tawdry and bizarre. The tones and shades, modest and tender, subdued yet rich, in which his fancy had always taken special delight, would be the ones which are conspicuously absent. But time would bring a gradual change. Some day he would suddenly become conscious that outlines which at first seemed harsh and trivial have grace and meaning; that forms which seemed grotesque are full of dignity; that magnitudes which had added enormity to coarseness have become replete with strength and even majesty; that colors which had been esteemed unrefined, immodest, and glaring, are as expressive, tender, changeful, and capacious of effects as any others. Great innovations, whether in art or literature, in science or in nature, seldom take the world by storm. They must be understood before they can be estimated, and must be cultivated before they can be understood.

Amen. Dutton describes a process of westernization of the perceptions that has to happen before the West is beautiful to us. You have to get over the color green; you have to quit associating beauty with gardens and lawns; you have to get used to an inhuman scale; you have to understand geological time.

Painters of the West have been hunting a new palette for the western landscape, from Miller and Bodmer to Georgia O'Keeffe, Maynard Dixon, and Millard Sheets. They have been trying to see western landforms with a clear eye ever since the Baron von Egloffstein, illustrating the report of Lieutenant Ives, showed the Grand Canyon with rims like puffs of cloud, exaggerated its narrowness and depth, and showed nothing of what the trained eye sees first—the persistence of the level strata and the persistent profile of the cliffs. Writers have been trying to learn how to see, and have been groping for a vocabulary better than castles and silent sentinels, but often amateurs of a scientific bent, such as Dutton, have had to show them how. And audiences, taught partly by direct contact with the landscape and partly by studying its interpreters, have been slowly acquiring a set of perceptual habits and responses appropriate to western forms and colors. Perception, like art and literature, like history, is an artifact, a human creation, and it is not created overnight.

The Westerner is less a person than a continuing adaptation. The West is less a place than a process. And the western landscape that it has taken us a century and three quarters to learn about, and partially adapt our farming, our social institutions, our laws, and our aesthetic perceptions to, has now become our most valuable natural resource, as subject to raid and ruin as the more concrete resources that have suffered from our rapacity. We are in danger of becoming scenery sellers—and scenery is subject to as much enthusiastic overuse and overdevelopment as grass and water. It can lead us into an ill-considered crowding on the heels of our resources. Landscape, with its basis of aridity, is both our peculiar splendor and our peculiar limitation. Without careful controls and restrictions and planning, tourists can be as destructive as locusts—can destroy everything we have learned to love about the West. I include you and me among the tourists, and I include you and me in my warning to entrepreneurs. We should all be forced to file an environmental impact study before we build so much as a privy or a summer cottage, much less a motel, a freeway, or a resort.

Sometimes I wonder if Lewis and Clark shouldn't have been made to file an environmental impact study before they started west, and Columbus before he ever sailed. They might never have got their permits. But then we wouldn't have been here to learn from our mistakes, either. I really only want to say that we may love a place and still be dangerous to it. We ought to file that environmental impact study before we undertake anything that exploits or alters or endangers the splendid, spacious, varied, magnificent, and terribly fragile earth that supports us. If we can't find an appropriate government agency with which to file it, we can file it where an Indian would have filed it—with our environmental conscience, our slowly maturing sense that the earth is indeed our mother, worthy of our love and deserving of our care. That may be the last stage of our adaptation to the western landscape, and it may come too late.

Idah Meacham Strobridge

From "The Lure of the Desert" in
In Miner's Mirage-Land

Except you are kindred with those who have speech with great spaces, and the Four Winds of the earth, and the infinite arch of God's sky, you shall not have understanding of the Desert's lure.

It is not the Desert's charm that calls one. What is it? I know not; only that there is a low, insistent voice calling—calling—calling. Not a loud voice. The Desert proclaiming itself, speaks gently. And we—every child of us who has laid on the breast of a mother while she rocked slowly, and hushed our fretting with a soft-sung lullaby song—we know how a low voice soothes and lulls one into sleep.

You are tired of the world's ways? Then, if you and the Desert have found each other, surely you will feel the drawing of your soul toward the eternal calm—the brooding peace that is there in the gray country.

Does the beautiful in Nature thrill you to your fingertips? When your eye is so trained that it may discover the beauty that dwells in that vast, still corner of the world, and your ear is attuned to catch the music of the plains or the anthems sung in deep cañons by the winds; when your heart finds comradeship in the mountains and the great sand-seas, the sun and the stars, and the huge cloud-drifts that the Desert winds set a-rolling round the world— when all these reach your heart by way of your eye and your ear, then you shall find one of the alluring ways that belongs to the Desert.

Do you seek for the marvelous? Or do you go a-quest for riches? Or simply desire to wander away into little known rifts in the wilderness? By these lures and a hundred others will the Desert draw you there. And once there, unprejudiced, the voice by and by will make itself heard as it whispers at your ear. And when you can lay your head on its breast, and hear its heart-beats, you will know a rest that is absolute and infinite. Then, you will understand those who yearly go a-searching for the mythical mines of mirage-land, and those who have lived apart from others for a lifetime, and are forgot by all their kindred and friends of a half-century ago. You will say: "It is the Desert's lure—I know—they cannot help it. And—yes!—it is worth all the penalty the gray land makes them pay!"

If you go to the Desert, and live there, you learn to love it. If you go away, you will never forget it for one instant in after life; it will be with you in memory forever and forever. And always will you hear the still voice that lures one, calling—and calling.

Terry Tempest Williams

"Peregrine Falcon" in
Refuge: An Unnatural History of Family and Place

Not far from Great Salt Lake is the municipal dump.
Acres of trash heaped high. Depending on your
frame of mind, it is either an olfactory fright show
or a sociological gold mine. Either way, it is best to
visit in winter.

For the past few years, when the Christmas Bird
Count comes around, I seem to be relegated to the
landfill. The local Audubon hierarchy tell me I am
sent there because I know gulls. The truth lies
deeper. It's an under-the-table favor. I am sent to
the dump because secretly they know I like it.

As far as birding goes, there's often no place better. Our urban wastelands are becoming wildlife's
last stand. The great frontier. We've moved them
out of town like all other "low-income tenants."

The dump where I count birds for Christmas used to have cattails—but I can't remember them. A few have popped up below the hill again, in spite of the bulldozers, providing critical cover for coots, mallards, and a variety of other waterfowl. I've seen herons standing by and once a snowy egret, but for the most part, the habitat now is garbage, perfect for starlings and gulls.

I like to sit on the piles of unbroken Hefties, black bubbles of sanitation. It provides comfort with a view. Thousands of starlings cover refuse with their feet. Everywhere I look—feathered trash.

The starlings gorge themselves, bumping into each other like drunks. They are not discretionary. They'll eat anything, just like us. Three starlings picked a turkey carcass clean. Afterward, they crawled inside and wore it as a helmet. A carcass with six legs walking around—you have to be sharp counting birds at the dump.

I admire starlings' remarkable adaptability. Home is everywhere. I've seen them nesting under awnings on New York's Fifth Avenue, as well as inside aspen trunks in the Teton wilderness. Over 50 percent of their diet is insects. They are the most effective predators against the clover weevil in America.

Starlings are also quite beautiful if looked at with beginner's eyes. In autumn and winter, their plumage appears speckled, unkempt. But by spring, the lighter tips of their feathers have been worn away, leaving them with a black, glossy plumage, glistening with irridescences.

Inevitably, students at the museum will describe an elegant, black bird with flashes of green, pink, and purple.

"About this big," they say (holding their hands about seven inches apart vertically). "With a bright yellow bill. What is it?"

"A starling," I answer.

What follows is a dejected look flushed with embarrassment.

"Is that all?"

The name precedes the bird.

I understand it. When I'm out at the dump with starlings, I don't want to like them. They are common. They are aggressive, and they behave poorly, crowding out other birds. When a harrier happens to cross-over from the marsh, they swarm him. He disappears. They want their trash to themselves.

Perhaps we project on to starlings that which we deplore in ourselves: our numbers, our aggression, our greed, and our cruelty. Like starlings, we are taking over the world.

The parallels continue. Starlings forage by day in open country competing with native species such as bluebirds for food. They drive them out. In late afternoon, they return in small groups to nest elsewhere, competing with cavity nesters such as flickers, martins, tree swallows, and chickadees. Once again, they move in on other birds' territories.

Starlings are sophisticated mimics singing songs of bobwhites, killdeer, flickers, and phoebes. Their flocks drape bare branches in spring with choruses of chatters, creeks, and coos. Like any good impostor, they confuse the boundaries. They lie.

What is the impact of such a species on the land? Quite simply, a loss of diversity.

What makes our relationship to starlings even more curious is that we loathe them, calling in exterminators because we fear disease, yet we do everything within our power to encourage them as we systematically erase the specialized habitats of specialized birds. I have yet to see a snowy egret spearing a bagel.

The man who wanted Shakespeare's birds flying in Central Park and altruistically brought starlings to America from England, is not to blame. We are—for creating more and more habitat for a bird we despise. Perhaps the only value in the multitudes of starlings we have garnished is that in some small way they allow us to comprehend what vast flocks of birds must have felt like.

The symmetry of starling flocks takes my breath away, I lose track of time and space. At the dump, all it takes is the sweep of my hand. They rise. Hundreds of starlings. They wheel and turn, twist and glide, with no apparent leader. They are the collective. A flight of frenzy. They are black stars against a blue sky. I watch them above the dump, expanding and contracting along the meridian of a winged universe.

Suddenly, the flock pulls together like a winced eye, then opens in an explosion of feathers. A peregrine falcon is expelled, but not without its prey. With folded wings he strikes a starling and plucks its body from mid-air. The flock blinks again and the starlings disperse, one by one, returning to the landfill.

The starlings at the Salt Lake City municipal dump give us numbers that look good on our Christmas Bird Count, thousands, but they become faceless when compared to one peregrine falcon. A century ago, he would have seized a teal.

I will continue to count birds at the dump, hoping for under-the-table favors, but don't mistake my motives. I am not contemplating starlings. It is the falcon I wait for—the duckhawk with a memory for birds that once blotted out the sun.

Henry David Thoreau

From "Solitude" in *Walden*

This is a delicious evening, when the whole body is one sense, and imbibes delight through every pore. I go and come with a strange liberty in Nature, a part of herself. As I walk along the stony shore of the pond in my shirt-sleeves, though it is cool as well as cloudy and windy, and I see nothing special to attract me, all the elements are unusually congenial to me. The bullfrogs trump to usher in the night, and the note of the whip-poor-will is borne on the rippling wind from over the water. Sympathy with the fluttering alder and poplar leaves almost takes away my breath; yet, like the lake, my serenity is rippled but not ruffled. These small waves raised by the evening wind are as remote from storm as the smooth reflecting surface. Though it is now dark, the wind still blows and roars in the wood, the waves still dash, and some creatures lull the rest with their notes. The repose is never complete. The wildest animals do not repose, but seek their prey now; the fox, and skunk, and rabbit, now roam the fields and woods without fear. They are Nature's watchmen,—links which connect the days of animated life.

When I return to my house I find that visitors have been there and left their cards, either a bunch of flowers, or a wreath of evergreen, or a name in pencil on a yellow walnut leaf or a chip. They who come rarely to the woods take some little piece of the forest into their hands to play with by the way, which they leave, either intentionally or accidentally. One has peeled a willow wand, woven it into a ring, and dropped it on my table. I could always tell if visitors had called in my absence, either by the bended twigs or grass, or the print of their shoes, and generally of what sex or age or quality they were by some slight trace left, as a flower dropped, or a bunch of grass plucked and thrown away, even as far off as the railroad, half a mile distant, or by the lingering odor of a cigar or pipe. Nay, I was frequently notified of the passage of a traveler along the highway sixty rods off by the scent of his pipe.

There is commonly sufficient space about us. Our horizon is never quite at our elbows. The thick wood is not just at our door, nor the pond, but somewhat is always clearing, familiar and worn by us, appropriated and fenced in some way, and re-claimed from Nature. For what reason have I this vast range and circuit, some square miles of unfre-quented forest, for my privacy, abandoned to me by men? My nearest neighbor is a mile distant, and no house is visible from any place but the hill-tops within half a mile of my own. I have my horizon bounded by woods all to myself; a distant view of the railroad where it touches the pond on the one hand, and of the fence which skirts the woodland road on the other. But for the most part it is as soli-tary where I live as on the prairies. It is as much Asia or Africa as New England. I have, as it were, my own sun and moon and stars, and a little world all to myself. At night there was never a traveler passed my house, or knocked at my door, more than if I were the first or last man; unless it were in the spring, when at long intervals some came from the village to fish for pouts,—they plainly fished much more in the Walden Pond of their own natures, and baited their hooks with darkness,—but they soon retreated, usually with light baskets, and left "the world to darkness and to me," and the black kernel of the night was never profaned by any human neighborhood. I believe that men are generally still a little afraid of the dark, though the witches are all hung, and Christianity and candles have been introduced.

Yet I experienced sometimes that the most sweet and tender, the most innocent and encouraging society may be found in any natural object, even for the poor misanthrope and most melancholy man. There can be no very black melancholy to him who lives in the midst of nature and has his senses still. There was never yet such a storm but it was Æolian music to a healthy and innocent ear. Nothing can rightly compel a simple and brave man to a vulgar sadness. While I enjoy the friendship of the seasons I trust that nothing can make life a burden to me. The gentle rain which waters my beans and keeps me in the house today is not drear and melancholy, but good for me too. Though it prevents my hoeing them, it is of far more worth than my hoeing. If it should continue so long as to cause the seeds to rot in the ground and destroy the potatoes in the low lands, it would still be good for the grass on the uplands, and, being good for the grass, it would be good for me. Sometimes, when I compare myself with other men, it seems as if I were more favored by the gods than they, beyond any deserts that I am conscious of; as if I had a warrant and surety at their hands which my fellows have not, and were especially guided and guarded. I do not flatter myself, but if it be possible they flatter me. I have never felt lonesome, or in the least oppressed by a sense of solitude, but once, and that was a few weeks after I came to the woods, when, for an hour, I doubted if the near neighborhood of man was not essential to a serene and healthy life. To be alone was something unpleasant. But I was at the same time conscious of a light insanity in my mood, and seemed to foresee my recovery. In the midst of a gentle rain while these thoughts prevailed, I was suddenly sensible of such sweet and beneficent society in Nature, in the very pattering of the drops, and in every sound and sight around my house, an infinite and unaccountable friendliness all at once like an atmosphere sustaining me, as made the fancied advantages of human neighborhood insignificant, and I have never thought of them since. Every little pine needle expanded and swelled with sympathy and befriended me. I was so distinctly made aware of the presence of something kindred to me, even in scenes which we are accustomed to call wild and dreary, and also that the nearest of blood to me and humanest was not a person nor a villager, that I thought no place could ever be strange to me again.—

> "*Mourning untimely consumes the sad;*
> *Few are their days in the land of the living,*
> *Beautiful daughter of Toscar.*"

Some of my pleasantest hours were during the long rainstorms in the spring or fall, which confined me to the house for the afternoon as well as the forenoon, soothed by their ceaseless roar and pelting; when an early twilight ushered in a long evening in which many thoughts had time to take root and unfold themselves. In those driving northeast rains which tried the village houses so, when the maids stood ready with mop and pail in front entries to keep the deluge out, I sat behind my door in my little house, which was all entry, and thoroughly enjoyed its protection. In one heavy thundershower the lightning struck a large pitch pine across the pond, making a very conspicuous and perfectly regular spiral groove from top to bottom, an inch or more deep, and four or five inches wide, as you would groove a walking-stick. I passed it again the other day, and was struck with awe on looking up and beholding that mark, now more distinct than ever, where a terrific and resistless bolt came down out of the harmless sky eight years ago. Men frequently say to me, "I should think you would feel lonesome down there, and want to be nearer to folks, rainy and snowy days and nights especially." I am tempted to reply to such,—This whole earth which we inhabit is but a point in space. How far apart, think you, dwell the two most distant inhabitants of yonder star, the breadth of whose disk cannot be appreciated by our instruments? Why should I feel lonely? Is not our planet in the Milky Way? This which you put seems to me not to be the most important question. What sort of space is that which separates a man from his fellows and makes him solitary? I have found that no exertion of the legs can bring two minds much nearer to one another. What do we want most to dwell near to? Not to many men surely, the depot, the post-office, the bar-room, the meeting-house, the school-house, the grocery, Beacon Hill, or the Five Points, where men most congregate, but to the perennial source of our life, whence in all our experience we have found that to issue, as the willow stands near the water and sends out its roots in that direction. This will vary with different natures, but this is the place where a wise man will dig his cellar. . . .I one evening overtook one of my townsmen, who has accumulated what is called "a handsome property,"—though I never got a fair view of it,—on the Walden road, driving a pair of cattle to market, who inquired of me how I could bring my mind to give up so many of the comforts of life. I answered that I was very sure I liked it passably well; I was not joking. And so I went home to my bed, and left him to pick his way through the darkness and the mud to Brighton,—or Bright-town,—which place he would reach some time in the morning.

Henry David Thoreau

From "Visitors" in *Walden*

Every morning was a cheerful invitation to make my life of equal simplicity, and I may say innocence, with Nature herself. I have been as sincere a worshipper of Aurora as the Greeks. I got up early and bathed in the pond; that was a religious exercise, and one of the best things which I did. They say that characters were engraven on the bathing tub of King Tching-thang to this effect: "Renew thyself completely each day; do it again, and again, and forever again." I can understand that. Morning brings back the heroic ages. I was as much affected by the faint hum of a mosquito making its invisible and unimaginable tour through my apartment at earliest dawn, when I was sitting with door and windows open, as I could be by any trumpet that

ever sang of fame. It was Homer's requiem; itself
and Iliad and Odyssey in the air, singing its own
wrath and wanderings. There was something
cosmical about it; a standing advertisement, till
forbidden, of the everlasting vigor and fertility of
the world. The morning, which is the most memorable season of the day, is the awakening hour. Then
there is least somnolence in us; and for an hour, at
least, some part of us awakes which slumbers all
the rest of the day and night. Little is to be expected
of that day, if it can be called a day, to which we are
not awakened by our Genius, but by the mechanical nudgings of some servitor, are not awakened by
our own newly acquired force and aspirations from
within, accompanied by the undulations of celestial music, instead of factory bells, and a fragrance
filling the air—to a higher life than we fell asleep
from; and thus the darkness bear its fruit, and prove
itself to be good, no less than the light. That man
who does not believe that each day contains an earlier, more sacred, and auroral hour than he has yet
profaned, has despaired of life, and is pursuing a
descending and darkening way. After a partial ces-
sation of his sensuous life, the soul of man, or its

organs rather, are reinvigorated each day, an his
Genius tries again what noble life it can make. All
memorable events, I should say, transpire in morning time and in a morning atmosphere. The Vedas
say, "All intelligences awake with the morning."
Poetry and art, and the fairest and most memorable of the actions of men, date from such an hour.
All poets and heroes, like Memnon, are the children of Aurora, and emit their music at sunrise. To
him whose elastic and vigorous thought keeps pace
with the sun, the day is a perpetual morning. It
matters not what the clocks say or the attitudes and
labors of men. Morning is when I am awake and
there is a dawn in me. Moral reform is the effort to
throw off sleep. Why is it that men give so poor an
account of their day if they have not been slumbering? They are not such poor calculators. If they
had not been overcome by drowsiness, they would
have performed something. The millions are awake
enough for physical labor; but only one in a million is awake enough for effective intellectual exertion, only one in a hundred millions to a poetic or
divine life. To be awake is to be alive. I have never
yet met a man who was quite awake. How could I

have looked him in the face?

We must learn to reawaken and keep ourselves awake, not by mechanical aids, but by an infinite expectation of the dawn, which does not forsake us in our soundest sleep. I know of no more encouraging fact than the unquestionable ability of man to elevate his life by a conscious endeavor. It is something to be able to paint a particular picture, or to carve a statue, and so to make a few objects beautiful; but it is far more glorious to carve and paint the very atmosphere and medium through which we look, which morally we can do. To affect the quality of the day, that is the highest of arts. Every man is tasked to make his life, even in its details, worthy of the contemplation of his most elevated and critical hour. If we refused, or rather used up, such paltry information as we get, the oracles would distinctly inform us how this might be done.

I went to the woods because I wished to live deliberately, to front only the essential facts of life, and see if I could not learn what it had to teach, and not, when I came to die, discover that I had not lived. I did not wish to live what was not life, living is so dear; nor did I wish to practice resignation, unless it was quite necessary. I wanted to live deep and suck out all the marrow of life, to live so sturdily and Spartan-like as to put to rout all that was not life, to cut a broad swath and shave close, to drive life into a corner, and reduce it to its lowest terms, and, if it proved to be mean, why then to get the whole and genuine meanness of it, and publish its meanness to the world; or if it were sublime, to know it by experience, and be able to give a true account of it in my next excursion. For most men, it appears to me, are in a strange uncertainty about it, whether it is of the devil or of God, and have *somewhat hastily* concluded that it is the chief end of man here to "glorify God and enjoy him forever."

Still we live meanly, like ants; though the fable tells us that we were long ago changed into men; like pygmies we fight with cranes; it is error upon error, and clout upon clout, and our best virtue has for its occasion a superfluous and evitable wretchedness. Our life is frittered away by detail. An honest man had hardly need to count more than his ten fingers, or in extreme cases he may add his ten toes, and lump the rest. Simplicity, simplicity, simplicity! I say, let your affairs be as two or three, and not a hundred or a thousand; instead of a million count half a dozen, and keep your accounts on your thumb-nail. In the midst of this chopping sea of civilized life, such are the clouds and storms and quicksands and thousand-and-one items to be allowed for, that a man has to live, if he would not founder and go to the bottom and not make his port at all, by dead reckoning, and he must be a great calculator indeed who succeeds. Simplify, simplify.

Walt Whitman

From "A Song of the Rolling Earth" in
Leaves of Grass

3

I swear the earth shall surely be complete to him or
    her who shall be complete,
The earth remains jagged and broken only to him
    or her who remains jagged and broken.

I swear there is no greatness or power that does
    not emulate those of the earth,
There can be no theory of any account unless it
    corroborate the theory of the earth,
No politics, song, religion, behavior, or what not,
    is of account, unless it compare with the ampli-
    tude of the earth,
Unless it face the exactness, vitality, impartiality,
    rectitude of the earth.

I swear I begin to see love with sweeter spasms than
    that which responds love,
It is that which contains itself, which never invites
    and never refuses.

I swear I begin to see little or nothing in audible
    words,
All merges toward the presentation of the unspo-
    ken meanings of the earth,
Toward him who sings the songs of the body and
    of the truths of the earth,
Toward him who makes the dictionaries of words
    that print cannot touch.

I swear I see what is better than to tell the best,
It is always to leave the best untold.

When I undertake to tell the best I find I cannot,
My tongue is ineffectual on its pivots,
My breath will not be obedient to its organs,
I become a dumb man.

The best of the earth cannot be told anyhow, all or
    any is best,

It is not what you anticipated, it is cheaper, easier,
    nearer,
Things are not dismiss'd from the places they held
    before,
The earth is just as positive and direct as it was be-
    fore,
Facts, religions, improvements, politics, trades, are
    as real as before,
But the soul is also real, it too is positive and direct,
No reasoning, no proof has establish'd it,
Undeniable growth has establish'd it.

Ann Zwinger

From "Turk's Head to the Confluence" in
*Run, River, Run: A Naturalist's Journey Down One
of the Great Rivers of the West*

A SAND BAR marks the turn of the inner cliff,
rimmed with an abatis of tamarisk below a loose
gray limestone slope. I work up the steep incline,
slipping and grabbing, mostly air. There is little to
hold to and often, in sneakers, two steps up are suc-
ceeded by three steps down. The slope is surfaced
with treacherous scree and the limestone is hard
on the hands. There are many crinoid stems all over
the ground, each slightly different, serrated or
smooth, centered with a round channel or a five-
lobed one, each of which deserves to be minutely
examined before being returned to its impression
in the dirt. Attaining the high ledge above me becomes a test, a race against time, while the light

holds, before this day drifts downstream. The ledge, when I reach it, is just wide enough to hunker on, back against the slope. Facing the paired cliff across the river, I feel like some small animal, protected, nestled safely above predator below. But a sense of uneasiness assails me as a hawk drifts over and then comes in lower for a second pass.

I am sad, depressed. These are feelings that do not come often on the river. I remember the next to the last trip for this book, down Desolation Canyon. I awoke at first light with foreboding, torn unwillingly out of sleep by the carping of a magpie. As the sky grew light, I unzipped the tent fly and clipped it back. The big bird teetered on a beached snag, switching its long tail, voice harsh and wheedling. Across the river, the east-facing cliffs caught first light—pale peach, the color of the inside of a conch shell. As I watched, the color warmed faintly, and the river carried cream and gold and apricot in thin undulating lines. For the first time I felt out of phase with the light, with the clarity of a river morning.

I took extra time with the tent, wiped it more carefully than usual, wedged the damp sand out of my boot cleats, took solace in quiet tasks and busy hands. And, when all these things were done, I turned my back on the river and walked the sand bar. It lay wide, sprigged with thousands of green tamarisks two or three inches high. Where silt had dried, it curled up in uneven plates. A last sunflower bloomed, knee-high, with frost spots on the petals. Facing the sun for whatever warmth there was, I wished it to soothe and heal. The furze of tamarisks shimmered with dew, but walking toward the sun, I was Die Frau ohne Schatten.

Without shadow—without all the familiar framework of my other world, in the self-imposed isolation of wilderness, I had found moments of nonrecordable time: the discovery of sinuous beauty in a point bar, the elegance of a meander, the challenge of running a rapid myself. The river had brought moments of elation that had come so unexpectedly that I could not breathe for the delight: a mockingbird at midnight in a quiet-rimmed canyon; the constellation Orion wheeling up at four in the morning, striding a misty sky over a misty river; the moon rising in a cool sidereal light, locked in star patterns, over an October-frosted sand bar;

a rim of white sandstone turning rose in afterglow. I admitted this necessity of solitude. When I turned to walk back to camp, I gained a shadow. It went before me, outlined by an opalescent aura of sun catching in prisms of dew. I walked into a glowing mandorla of aloneness, toward the river.

Now, below me, the gentle curve of the sand bar at the confluence stretches to velvet smoothness, a boomerang held tightly between cliff and river. At noon the light on this slope is so bright that I cannot look at the water without squinting, and the ripples shoot out flashes of retina-shattering light. The midday brilliance washes out colors and consumes shadows. But the light softens in late afternoon, gentles the wide-open dazzle of this landscape. It lessens the demands on eyesight and so brings an easing of muscle and mind. Even the river seems slower in its going as it creams into vortices and piles downstream, an optical illusion brought on by my own slowing metabolism. Human warmth slips out of skin into sand and only residual warmth in the rock preserves the bone against chilling. The river runs with soft ochre and evening reflections.

Across the river the matched cliff rises, split by
an unconformity that represents millions of years
of lost time. Some part of mental discipline notes
the logic of rock layers and light intensity and vortices of time and space, but something slips with
the river's going. Logic time crosses over to river
time. Time is only today on the river and tonight
on the sand bar. Days of the week have no meaning. Nor do eons or epochs. The cliff across the river
is as durable as the sand bar below, and the sand
bar lasts as long as the morning light on the cliff. I
remember how the river sounds as it melts six-
spoked silt-free crystals to pellucid drops, once oxy-
gen and twice hydrogen. And, as it rose in rock, so
it ends in rock, not in the hard, shattered gray gran-
ites, but the sediments from more ancient mountains, layered, worked, reworked, laid in witness
layers.

A cliff swallow makes a last sweep of the sky,
then shafts like an arrow downstream. The wind
stills. It is too quiet.

I do not want to hear the river ending.

About the Editor

A resident of Helena, Montana, since 1989, Amy Kelley grew up in a family of five girls in Madison, Wisconsin, where summer days were spent at the neighborhood pool and family vacations were spent camping. Rather than a serene wilderness experience, Amy recalls camping as a rowdy family affair, where telling stories around the campfire played an important role.

Since graduating from Oberlin College in 1983, Amy has worked primarily for various public interest organizations as an organizer, writer, publications designer, lobbyist, advocate, and illustrator. Her work experience has taken some interesting side jogs as well, including two seasons working at a fly-fishing lodge in southern Chile.

This anthology series was compiled over two years, during which time Amy left Helena to attend art school in Portland, Oregon. Now back in Helena, her freelance work life affords ample opportunity to take off into the mountains and Montana's open spaces for mountain biking, hiking, camping, and cross-country skiing.

The Adventure Series

Written or collected and edited by climber and adventurer John Long, each gripping story will keep both the adrenaline-driven participant and the armchair adventurer riveted.

Long on Adventure
The Best of John Long

The Big Drop
Classic Big Wave Surfing Stories

The High Lonesome
Epic Solo Climbing Stories

The Liquid Locomotive
Legendary Whitewater River Stories

To order these titles check with your local bookseller or call FALCON ® at **1-800-582-2665**
www.Falcon.com

FALCONGUIDES® Leading the Way™

PADDLING GUIDES
Paddling Minnesota
Paddling Montana
Paddling Okefenokee
Paddling Oregon
Paddling Yellowstone/Grand Teton

ROCK CLIMBING GUIDES
Rock Climbing Arizona
Rock Climbing Colorado
Rock Climbing Montana
Rock Climbing New Mexico & Texas
Rock Climbing Utah
Rock Climbing Washington

ROCKHOUNDING GUIDES
Rockhounding Arizona
Rockhounding California
Rockhounding Colorado
Rockhounding Montana
Rockhounding Nevada
Rockhound's Guide to New Mexico
Rockhounding Texas
Rockhounding Utah
Rockhounding Wyoming

BIRDING GUIDES
Birding Georgia
Birding Illinois
Birding Minnesota
Birding Montana
Birding Northern California
Birding Texas
Birding Utah

WALKING
Walking Colorado Springs
Walking Denver
Walking Portland
Walking San Francisco
Walking Seattle
Walking St. Louis
Walking Virginia Beach

FISHING GUIDES
Fishing Alaska
Fishing the Beartooths
Fishing Florida
Fishing Georgia
Fishing Glacier National Park
Fishing Maine
Fishing Montana
Fishing Wyoming
Fishing Yellowstone

Trout Unlimited's Guide to America's 100 Best
    Trout Streams
America's Best Bass Fishing

Field Guides
Alpine Wildflowers
Bitterroot: Montana State Flower
Canyon Country Wildflowers
Central Rocky Mountains Wildflowers
Chihuahuan Desert Wildflowers
Forest Wildflowers
Great Lakes Berry Book
Naturalist's Guide to Canyon Country
New England Berry Book
Northwest Penstemons
Ozark Wildflowers
Pacific Northwest Berry Book
Plants of Arizona
Plants of Rocky Mountain National Park
Prairie Wildflowers
Rare Plants of Colorado
Rocky Mountain Berry Book
Scats & Tracks of the Pacific Coast States
Scats & Tracks of the Rocky Mountains
Sierra Nevada Wildflowers
Southern Rocky Mountain Wildflowers
Tallgrass Prairie Wildflowers
Wayside Wildflowers of the Pacific Northwest
Western Trees
Wildflowers of Southwestern Utah

FALCON™

FALCON GUIDES ® Leading the Way™

www.Falcon.com

Since 1979, Falcon® has brought you the best in outdoor recreational guidebooks. Now you can access that same reliable and accurate information online.

❒ In-depth content, maps, and advice on a variety of outdoor activities, including hiking, climbing, biking, scenic driving, and wildlife viewing.

❒ A free monthly E-newsletter that delivers the latest news right to your inbox.

❒ Our popular games section where you can win prizes just by playing.

❒ An exciting and educational kids' section featuring online quizzes, coloring pages, and other activities.

❒ Outdoor forums where you can exchange ideas and tips with other outdoor enthusiasts.

❒ Also Falcon screensavers, online classified ads, and panoramic photos of spectacular destinations.

And much more!

Plan your next outdoor adventure at our website. Point your browser to www.Falcon.com and get FalconGuided!

FALCON®